BOOK OF ARIES

MAGIC OF ESSENTIAL MEANING

&

THE PATH OF BRILLIANCE

RAWN CLARK

© 2022

BOOK OF ARIES
By Rawn Clark

Dedication

The Universe has deemed it timely for me to release this Magic at this moment in time. It has truly taken me a lifetime of work, without any earthly guide, to learn how to present it to you in any kind of legible form. It feels important to our collective future that this magic arises within the world consciousness now, even though few will ever read my words. At least it is now a presence in the human collective awareness and I am certain that it will spread from here to become of importance as we seek to heal our planet in the future.

I dedicate this book to my e-friend and fellow Bardonist, J.M. – this one's for you! I also dedicate it to S., B., P.Y., F.B. and R. W. who have been my constant companions and without whom I could not have written.

CONTENTS

Introduction

I should start by saying (for those who don't already know), that I owe an infinitely large debt of gratitude to the Czech magician, Franz Bardon, who died just a few months after I was born. Sadly for me, I never had chance to meet him except through his books, foremost of which is his "Initiation Into Hermetics". I can only hope that this humble offering of mine achieves the sufficient quality to be accepted as an addition to Bardon's wonderful corpus of writings and sit along side of his works on evocation and kabbalah as exemplars of what comes next *after* IIH.

The main point or purpose of this book is to teach you the Magic of Essential Meaning but to get there; you must first learn to master the rainbow-hued Adonai Light and Kethric Brilliance. So we will go on a round-about journey, starting with a little preparatory work, then the Path of Brilliance and ending with truly one of the highest forms of magic in existence.

The Kethric Brilliance is the most sublime form of Light, the Light of all Lights, the progenitor of Light itself. It is formed as The "I" realizes that it exists as a unique Being; when "I" becomes "I am!". This shift in awareness appears as a brilliance beyond all other brilliances. It is the menstrum within which (or from which) Essential Meaning crystallizes. It has no color, yet it is all color.

In order for us to wield this Brilliance magically, we ourselves have to descend *as* The "I" into manifestation; we have to rise through all the layers of our awareness, from the physical, to the astral, to the temporal mental, to the eternal mental and finally to The "I", and then descend, bringing The "I" *with* us, till The "I" stands, fully aware, within the temporal physical moment. Then, in that moment, the Kethric Brilliance bursts forth from within us in limitless supply.

So our fist step along this path will be to learn how to consciously and quickly raise our awareness up to The "I" and to become The "I" ItSelf. Then we will learn how to descend with equal alacrity into the present moment of time-space as The "I" and with full awareness of all the parts of Self. And finally, we will learn how to corral the Kethric Brilliance and tame it to our needs.

Generally, in order to do this work you must have first completed Step Eight of Franz Bardon's IIH. Ideally, you are beginning this work concurrent with the work of Step Nine of IIH. For the vast majority of people the ability to generate the Kethric Brilliance will depend upon having an absolute astral *and* mental equilibrium of the Elements, absolute control of the Elements and Fluids, mastery of the Akasha and of one's three bodies, and finally, familiarity with one's Greater Self or "Holy Guardian Genius".

However, it must be noted that there will always be exceptions to these norms – those rare, extremely gifted individuals who come into this life already fully equipped for this work due to past life experiences. This is especially true these days but nonetheless rare. It is also theoretically possible to reach the aforementioned prerequisites by other means than Franz Bardon's IIH, though I can recommend no better, more certain a path than this.

So, before we get to the business of learning how to generate the Kethric Brilliance, here's more specific information about what the Kethric Brilliance is.

The Kethric Brilliance:

The term "Kethric Brilliance" refers to the unified, non-sequential, un-differentiated essential meaning of BEing experienced by The One Self in Chokmah / Wisdom. "Kethric" means "of Kether / Crown"; Kether / Crown being the Sephirot of The "I", The One Self or Unity. In this way we indicate that it emerges from Kether / Crown but does not exist within Kether / Crown. Within Kether / Crown, the-thing-that-becomes our Kethric Brilliance exists as pure BEing instead of

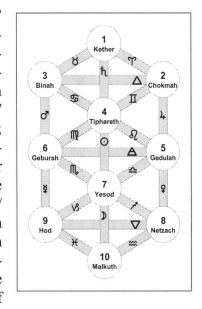

essential meaning -- it becomes un-differentiated essential meaning as it passes into Chokmah / Wisdom. This transformation of BEing into Meaning is symbolized by the zodiacal sign of Aries and the Hebrew Letter 'Heh' (ה).

We use the term "Brilliance" because within Chokmah / Wisdom it is more than just "Light" and yet it manifests many of the same qualities as Light such as radiance, penetration, illumination, etc. Our Kethric Brilliance encompasses *all* spectrums of "Light", as it were, *all* forms of meaning, *all* of BEing.

Within Chokmah / Wisdom, the un-differentiated essential meaning of BEing becomes Brilliance, or at least that is how our human awareness perceives this non-sequential, un-differentiated essential meaning. Here it is infinite in compass and content and it is singular in BEing. To say it "permeates all things" is to underestimate – it simply is all things. Or rather, all things are bits of it. Either way it is phrased, all things mental, astral and physical are composed of differentiated Kethric Brilliance. It is The Essential Substance, so to speak, The Prime Materia. It is the Awareness of The "I" experiencing the meaning of BEing. It is Life and Living, simultaneously.

As the Kethric Brilliance descends from Chokmah / Wisdom to Binah / Understanding it begins to differentiate, to transform from a unified wave-force into a unified particle-form. This transition from un-differentiation toward differentiation is symbolized by Archetypal Fire and the Hebrew Letter 'Shin' (ש).

Within Binah / Understanding, the Kethric Brilliance mixes with another emanation from Kether / Crown and becomes what we call "Akasha" in Bardonian Hermetics. This second "Kethric" influence is that of Form and the transformation of BEing into Embodiment is symbolized by the zodiacal sign of Taurus and the Hebrew Letter 'Vav' (ו). Akasha therefore is the intersection of un-differentiated meaning and the principle of embodiment – it is un-differentiated essential meaning that is in the process of differentiate-ing. Here there is infinite potential and infinite inevitability that each of those potentials is realized. The Akasha though is still a non-sequential state and true differentiation does not occur until we reach into the temporal realm of sequence and Tiphareth / Beauty where essential meaning assumes the Individualized form or Solitary Self.

Kethric Brilliance is an aspect of the Pillar of Force and Akasha, an aspect of the Pillar of Form. The focus of Akashic work is embodiment and transforming the nature of inevitable form; while work with the Kethric Brilliance is focused upon transforming the essential meaning embodied by form.

Since the Akasha is a form of Kethric Brilliance, it has specific characteristics and obeys specific "laws" and is in this way limited in comparison to the Kethric Brilliance. It cannot, for example be dynamically accumulated since it permeates all mental, astral and physical matter and thus cannot be constrained. It can be worked with but it cannot be substantially altered – the Akasha itself cannot be transformed into another substance such as an Element since the Akasha is a dynamic process of differentiate-ing. Akasha can only ever be Akasha even though all things emerge from the Akasha.

The Kethric Brilliance however is literally unlimited in all aspects. It can be willfully differentiated into any substance, shape, meaning form, etc. It can, by simple act of will, be dynamically accumulated or conversely, rendered a universal solvent that honors no barrier. It is easily manipulated with the creative imagination or will.

The Kethric Brilliance exists in its pure form at the level of Chokmah / Wisdom but it may also be "generated" at the mental, astral and physical levels. Since the Kethric Brilliance is the descending Awareness of The "I", it is naturally generated when a "lower" awareness is fully self-integrated and "brings" the Awareness of The "I" "down" into its own "lower" level of awareness. For example, when a human being integrates all the levels of its self-awareness, The "I" experiences the present moment of time-space as/through that human being and thus the Kethric Brilliance comes into existence in its pure form within that present moment of time-space. Once it has been "generated" in this way, it can then be put to specific use within that present moment of time-space.

So now, on to the matter of how to generate the Kethric Brilliance for yourself. First I will introduce you to the path we will be following on our "upward" journey:

The Structure:

Everything that exists shares a specific structure.

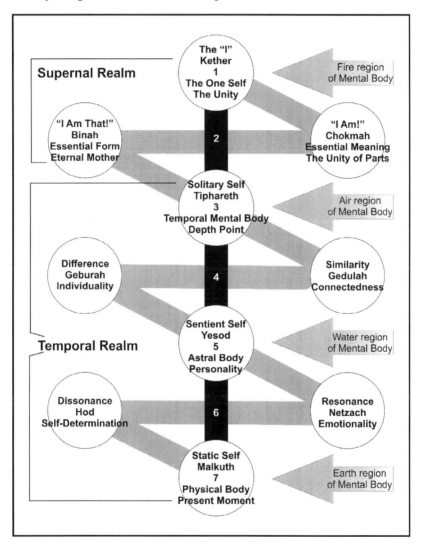

We will be using the pattern shown here -- the Kabbalistic (Gra) Tree of Life. It is an extremely accurate depiction of existence, both individual and Universal. Study it well and come to know it thoroughly as we will be constantly referring to it.

Pictured here is the pathway we will travel, from the most mundane level of our existence, to the most sublime -- from our physical body to The "I" ItSelf – and back again. We rise and we descend; but when we descend, we bring The "I" *with* us into the temporal present moment of time-space physical awareness and The "I" looks through our eyes, touches through our fingers, smells through our nose and speaks through our voice.

That – and only that – allows the Kethric Brilliance to emerge into the present moment. While the KB exists everywhere and within everything, it does so only in mixture and not in its pure form. What we are going to do here is manifest it in its *pure* form (where it does not usually exist) and in its pure form is where immeasurable magic power lies.

To truly tread this path we must first learn about it and prepare ourselves. Our education must begin at the beginning, with The "I". . .

<u>Preparation</u>

♈

Station #1: The "I"

Life is *the* most common thing in the universe. *Every* thing is alive, is filled with "I"ness. The speck of dust on my computer screen is alive and filled with "I"ness. The fly buzzing around my apartment is filled with "I"ness. The Camellia bush outside my door is filled with "I"ness. The Moon is filled with "I"ness. The small creature swimming about in some distant ocean on some distant planet circling some distant star is full of aliveness and possesses the same "I"ness. There is nothing that exists that is not alive and filled with "I"ness.

By "I"ness I mean the exact same sense of "I" that fills you, that sense of "I" you find when you look inside yourself and set aside your bias for the "me" and "mine". That universal "I" is Kether. It is the crown of existence. It is right there under the surface of you and of everything else that exists in the infinite universe.

"I" is *the* most common thing in the universe. This is why it is the first of the sephirot because it applies to *every* thing. It is supernal and universal, infinite and eternal in scope.

Cast your eyes around the space you are sitting in while you read and realize that *every* thing you see is *alive* and possesses "I"ness. Even the things we consider to be inanimate objects are alive with "I"ness. You are truly not alone... You are sitting in a sea of "I".

Practice:

1) Your first exercise is a meditation on The "I". Sit with your eyes closed and look within for The "I". It's not easy to find at first because all your false ideas as to what "I" is will get in the way. You must let go of all your preconceptions, let go of "me-ness" and all the limitations and personalizations of your ideas of "I".

Focus upon your *experience* of "I-ness", that sense and experience of simply being. Let go of everything except "I". You may want to make a mantra of "I", repeating the word over and over to focus your attention.

Carry on in this way until you can sit comfortably in The "I" for at least 5 minutes without interruption. This may take some weeks or months for you to achieve. In all cases you must be patient and persistent in equal measure.

This is a meditation for a lifetime and you should return to it often.

2) The second exercise in an extension of the first. Begin with your eyes closed as before and enter into The "I". Now cast your mind outward into your surroundings and sense The "I" in all things in your immediate environment.

Little by little expand the quantity of the universe included in the perception of "I". Grow your experience and perception of The "I" to include your block, your city, your country, your continent, your planet, your solar system, your galaxy, etc. until it encompasses the whole universe.

Feel The "I" as infinite . . . There is no differentiation to this "I". No "me", no "other", no parts, no individuals, only "I" — the One, Unified, Infinite Self.

Continue with this meditation until you can comfortably and quickly perceive this infinite "I".

3) This exercise is a departure from the previous two in that it is done with the eyes open. Sitting with your eyes open, immerse your mind in The "I" and look to your immediate surroundings. Let your eyes rest on one thing and perceive The "I" within it. Survey all the things within your immediate surroundings and perceive The "I" within each.

Now cast your eyes further afield perceiving The "I" within everything you see. You must perceive The "I" within the minutest thing and the largest thing equally.

Experiment in the different settings you encounter until you can easily and comfortably slip into this state of perception at any moment.

4) This exercise is an extension of the previous and is, as it were, a moving exercise. As you go throughout your day, recognize The "I" within each person, animal and thing you encounter. From your own place of perceiving The "I", greet The "I" within this other person/animal/object. You stand as equals, "I" to "I" . . .

Station #2: Essential Meaning & Essential Form

The "I" is self aware and recognizes itself as both an infinite singular self and as a self composed of an infinite number of parts.   It fills each part of itself equally with its essential meaning giving each part a life of its own. But The "I" is not a passive thing – it is expressive.

Each part, as well as the whole, actively expresses its essential meaning and it does so through form – through shape, size, color, duration, etc. So, in this sense, both form and essential meaning are also infinite and supernal.

Essential meaning always expresses itself through form and form is always an expression of essential meaning. Where there is life there is essential meaning and where there is form there is life.

Chokmah/Wisdom is essential meaning and Binah/ Understanding is form. In Chokmah we have the explosion of "I" into an infinite expanse of Kethric Brilliance which gives rise to an equally infinite expanse of Essential Meaning. In Binah we find the mother of all forms. Chokmah fills the womb of Binah with the fiery seed of essential meaning combined with the KB and Binah in turn gives a watery birth to the universe of things.

Essential meaning is at the same time a singular infinite thing and a particulate thing. There are an infinite number of different types of essential meaning just as there are an infinite number and variety of forms. Each form expresses either a single essential meaning or a combination of essential meanings, establishing infinite variety.

It is by looking though form that we directly perceive essential meaning. This direct perception results in an experiential "knowing" of the essence of the thing being examined; thus the title "wisdom" which is a deeper, more comprehensive and immediate thing than "understanding". We can attain an "understanding" of a thing by examining its structure but only when we look within its form do we arrive at the deeper state of "wisdom".

In Binah we find our Greater Self (or Holy Guardian Genius), our supernal mental body as it were. This is the Essential Meaning of ourselves.

Practice:

1) This first exercise will teach you how to directly perceive the essential meaning of any form.

Sit in a quiet place where you are assured of privacy. Choose five small objects and place them in front of you.

These objects can be anything so long as they are all markedly different from each other. For example, I have chosen five things from my immediate environment: a black cigarette lighter; a small statue of Ganesh; a pen; a clump of Spanish Moss; and, a small orange stone. They are all quite different from each other in appearance and function.

Now quiet your mind and gaze at each object in turn for a moment or two. Now look again at each object but this time try to perceive how it makes you *feel*.

This is an ever so brief and immediate perception that comes *before* you begin to form any thoughts about the object. It is pre-rational. Thinking about the object and thinking about your feelings — even naming your feelings or the object — come *after* this brief perception. This is very important and it may take some time and effort for you to master so be patient and persistent with your self.

Repeat this with your five objects until you get the hang of it and can immediately perceive the essential meaning in each.

Now choose a different five objects and repeat the exercise until you have perceived the essential meaning in each. Consider this exercise a success when you are able to perceive the essential meaning of any object placed before you.

2) As before, sit in a quiet, private room and clear your mind. Now methodically, starting directly in front of you and going from one thing to the next around the room, look at each object in turn and perceive its essential meaning as before.

This exercise is a success when you can perceive the contents of your room as a whole and individually.

3) Now we will take this exercise outside into your normal life. Prepare yourself by taking a moment to quiet your mind and bring your focus into your body and into the present moment. When you are ready, enter the outdoors and go for a walk. Perceive the essential meaning of everything, every person and every being you encounter. Pay special attention to perceiving the essential meaning of the people you meet.

You walk amidst a sea of essential meaning.

Do not be surprised or discouraged if you are unable to maintain this level of direct perception for more than a few moments at a time. It can be quite disorienting or disconcerting at first but give it time and it will become easier with practice. You can count your work with this exercise a success when you are able to maintain this level of perception for as long as you want, whenever and wherever you want.

4) Next, you will strive to prolong your perception of each Essential Meaning that you observe. You must extend what is ordinarily the briefest of perceptions and learn to sit with the

pure EM for as long as you desire. From this exercise you will begin to recognize different types of EM.

5) Finally, you must sit yourself down in front of a mirror and seek to perceive your own essential meaning. First the EM of your physical form and on to the EM of your Greater Self.

A wise friend once told me: "The EM of your physical body is your personality; the EM of your personality is your Individuality; the EM of your Individuality is your Greater Self; and, the EM of your Greater Self is The "I"."

Station #3: The Solitary Self

Imagine, if you will, a beautiful radiant diamond set in 24k gold — this is Tiphareth/Beauty. Or, imagine a sparkling sun set in a field of planets — this is Tiphareth/Beauty. Tiphareth is the Solitary Self, birthed by Binah, set in an expansive universe of other Solitary Selves. It is the first, most basic level of manifestation — a Kether in miniature as it were. As a concept, it symbolizes both a single Solitary Self and the entire infinite realm of Solitary Selves. It is your own temporal mental body and the temporal mental bodies of all that exists.

Each Solitary Self that makes up the infinite realm of Solitary Selves is distinctly unique in its own right. Yet each is similar to every other Solitary Self in that it has the same basic structure — a core of a specific, utterly unique combination of essential meaning, expressing itself by radiating its meaning outwards. We (every one of us) are, after all, just essential meaning expressing itself, as it must . . .

It is called "solitary" because it has a self contained "I-ness" that experiences itself as separate. It is a single, utterly unique unit of "I-ness" within an infinite ocean of "other".

Tiphareth is the level of self that incarnates over and over into material form, gaining experience as it goes, changing and growing with time. It is the core of who you are as a living, breathing human being.

Every thing that exists has a Tiphareth. The molecule of air you just inhaled has a Tiphareth; the plant in the pot on your windowsill has a Tiphareth; in fact, the cigarette lighter from our earlier experiment has a Tiphareth too. *Every* thing has a Tiphareth at its core.

As a human being your Tiphareth contains your all of your core traits that incarnate with slight differences during each of your lifetimes. It is also the reservoir of all the memories of your experiences from those innumerable lifetimes. And, it holds a record of all your various personalities and accomplishments from your long past. The Solitary Self is like a radiant sun shining its light upon all the circumstances of your life and the attributes of your incarnate personality.

And yet it exists only in the present moment of the NOW — the infinite NOW in which *every* thing exists. In other words, it experiences NOW as an infinite and unending thing.

It is the active part of you that lives life. It is the part of you that ultimately thinks and feels; or in non-human terms, it is that part of every thing that responds to, and interacts with the surrounding universe. It is why gold is recognizable as gold with its yellowish shine, instead of the red of iron or blue of tin. Ultimately, it is what makes each thing what it is, what makes you who you are, as distinct from what makes me who I am.

Tiphareth is the Depth Point of each thing.

Practice:

1) As an advanced student of Franz Bardon's IIH, you are well familiar with your Depth Point and the confines of your own mental body so there is no special practice required at this juncture in your understanding of this station along the path. In any event, what is necessary for our present needs is that you are able to identify your own awareness, perceive your own Depth Point and perceive the Depth Point of others.

Station #4: Alikeness & Difference

Consciousness is addicted to collectivism. Even though the Solitary Self is a lone thing that recognizes "other" and "self" as separate things, it still prefers to be part of a collective awareness. It's as if the Solitary Self has such fond memories of its time in the womb of Binah, connected to all its sisters and brothers, that it seeks out similar circumstances by becoming part of a collective of Solitary Selves.

Collectives come in all sizes and in all flavors and shapes. The only common factor in all collectives is a *similarity* or sameness of the Solitary Selves involved. This is to say, that there must be a commonality, or harmony, of essential meanings that compose the Solitary Selves involved, in order for them to be drawn together. "Like attracts like" is the rule when it comes to consciousness.

But, this does not necessarily mean that opposites repel each other. Picture if you will, an infinite continuum of alikeness where on one end, everything is 100% alike and on the other end they are 0% like the start of the line. *But*, there is the infinite continuum of alikeness by which the one end can find a path of relative alikeness to the other end! They are distant cousins, so to speak. Their differences are superceded by the fact they are part of a *continuum* of alikeness.

This brings us to the collective consciousness formed by whole infinite number of Solitary Selves . . . This is the supreme, universal collective whose needs overrule all lesser needs. Some examples of lesser collective awarenesses are the galactic collective, involving all the Solitary Selves that reside in that region of space-time; the stellar collective; the planetary collective; the species collective; the national, state, then city collective; the interest collective; the belief collective; the family collective; etc.

While it is alikeness which drawn collectives together, it is difference which forces them apart. For example two countries are at war with each other because of a difference in politics or religion, even though the citizens of both countries actually have more in common than not. At times the differences outweigh the commonalities and at other times they don't, but there is *always* that contention between alikeness and difference.

There is a different sort of power in both ends of this continuum of similarity and difference. The collective is the more powerful by far and most often supercedes the individual, yet it is at the individual scale that the true, inherent, unique power of each individual is revealed. Of course, that power is only relevant *within* the context of a collective. For example, you might be a powerful magician but unless you are doing something good for the world with your magic powers, it means absolutely nothing . . . it's just an "ego trip".

Each type of consciousness has different powers. For example a human consciousness has different powers than that of gold or an insect, etc. This of course is down to the types of essential meaning that comprise a human Solitary Self. Human consciousness, in contrast to that of gold, is very mobile and plastic, it can go anywhere and take on any form; whereas, gold consciousness is immobile and unchangeable.

So with Gedulah, all things are connected to each other by virtue of their all being composed of Essential Meaning. With Geburah however, everything is unique and has its own specific powers, and is therefore different from everything else. Of course, the very fact that every thing is unique is what they all have in common – forming an infinite loop of alikeness! LOL

Practice:

1) Again, as an advanced student of IIH who is comfortable transferring your awareness into any other thing or being, you already know the ways in which consciousness can unite with other awarenesses. And, of course, you are already acutely aware of your own unique attributes, powers and special abilities and are capable of using them to their fullest. Consequently, there are no special exercises you need to do for this station along the path. You need merely note your connectedness to all things and your simultaneous uniqueness.

Station #5: The Sentient Self

As a consequence of the Solitary Self learning its own unique power within the collective, a new level of awareness emerges — the Sentient Self. This is Yesod / Foundation, literally the foundation of the material realm. This is the incarnating self which exists in a milieu of *significance* where every thing and every event has a relative personal importance. Here the senses become activated and the relative importance of every thing in the Self's environment is *perceived*.

The Sentient Self is flooded with information about the *personal* relationship between self and environment, self and "other". The whole attention of the Sentient Self is wrapped up in this world of sensation and feeling or, in human terms, emotion. This is the astral realm and your Sentient Self in nothing other than your all too familiar astral body.

This realm is the template for the physical — it is this inner significance which eventually creates physicality. In order for essential meaning to become physical *it must first gain a very strong charge of significance and importance*, and this is the realm where that happens. Every Solitary Self is experiencing the significance of every other Solitary Self (i.e., every thing that exists), and in this way everything is given enough weight of significance and importance that it eventually becomes physical. In essence, the material world is created here in the astral and mirrors all astral things and events. Every physical thing has an astral "body", as it were, for without one, *it would not be significant enough to be physical*.

The Sentient Self is the self that interacts with "other". It *perceives* the significance of each "other" thing and then *evaluates* it, *judges* it and then *reacts* with a significance of its own — always in that order. Perceive, evaluate, judge, react, over and over, continuously building significance. These of course are the actions of the personality which, as you know, is also an aspect of the astral body.

31

Practice:

1) What is important for passage though this station along your journey is that you note your own personality and sense your own astral body. You must *feel* the energetic presence of your astral body -- just as when you are astral wandering -- but *within* your physical body instead of separate from it.

If you are not already familiar with the sensations of your astral body through the practice of astral wandering then you will need to gain this ability before proceeding.

Station #6: Resonance & Dissonance

Resonance.   That is the rule in the world of the Sentient Selves.   For the Solitary Selves the rule was "like attracts like" but here, it's not so simple.   Here, everything affects everything else through attraction and repulsion.   Or, more accurately put, through resonance and dissonance.

"Everything vibrates" because of interaction — they don't "vibrate" on their own — they vibrate *because* they are not alone and *must* resonate.   And with resonance comes perception . . .

Perception is not just a passive thing – it is an interaction between the perceiver and the perceived.   When a Sentient Self perceives, it is changed by its perception.   It slowly becomes, to some degree or another, what it perceives.   It resonates *with* the object of perception and is thereby changed -- just as when you see something funny, you smile and laugh and are made happier.

Each and every interaction changes us to some degree.   For a moment, our sense of "self" becomes more fluid as we empathize with "other".   That is, until we reach an indefinable moment when the changes become just a bit too extreme and we retreat into our more familiar borders of "self" -- we open and close.

The reason we close down is due to dissonance.   As we change, the difference between our "selves" and the "other" becomes too slender and we feel a sense of dissonance, of too much "otherness" creeping in, and we recoil in response.   This is a natural function of what we humans call "the self-preservation instinct".   It protects us from losing our own sense of "self".

This closing action strengthens the borders of our sense of "self", distinguishing us much more firmly as a unique person. It defines us as 'me' as opposed to "them". Resonance, on the other hand, expands our "self"; it increases the parameters of what we think of as "self". It adds to our definition of "self" making for a much more inclusive "me". We *grow* through resonance and *strengthen* through dissonance.

We have the power to use resonance and dissonance to manipulate our environment. For example, I might wear purple to attract a certain type of person who resonates with that color; or, I might wear scruffy, smelly clothes to alienate everyone. There are too many conscious and unconscious ways that we use this power to be worth enumerating!

The power behind resonance is what we humans think of as "love" — that overwhelming sense of attraction and desire to merge with another thing that has much the same content of essential meaning as we do. It is a very primal force so we naturally rush into it with open arms — "love" demands that we open to it.

The power behind dissonance is quite different. In human terms it is discernment. Discernment is much more intellectual than it is primal, though it is still an aspect of self-preservation. It is also much more individual, based upon the individual's life experiences, personal feelings and judgments.

Dissonance halts resonance, and conversely, resonance breaks down dissonance. Unrestrained by dissonance, resonance would break down all barriers of "self" and we would be left with an undifferentiated puddle of Self! And without resonance to intervene, dissonance would render us immobile and unchanging, incapable of interaction of any kind. Either way, the world would come crashing down because everything relies on a balance of these two forces.

By wielding resonance as if it were a tool (the Art of Resonance, so to speak), we can accomplish many things: we can open our selves to others and learn; we can manipulate our environment and others; and, most importantly of all, we can change ourselves. For example, if I want to be happy, I resonate with happiness; if I want another to be happy, I radiate happiness; and, if I want to comfort a friend, I begin by resonating with what they are feeling.

Dissonance, on the other hand, makes for an altogether different sort of tool. Its power as a tool is discernment. With discernment, we bring in the light of Wisdom and illuminate our understanding of things. We see them more clearly for what they are, instead of what we would like them to be. Discernment brings us into the moment and grounds us in reality, giving birth to our experience of the present moment. Discernment is the balancing of what we have learned from our experience of resonance; the integration of the lessons learned.

With resonance (Netzach / Vitality) we see and experience the emotional allure of it all and are ravished by its beauty. And by the powers of discernment (Hod / Splendor), we see and experience the overwhelmingly stupendous, magnificent splendor of it all as we peek into the workings of the universe . . .

Practice:

As before, there is no specific "practice" that needs doing at this stage in your own development. You will have done this long ago. For the purposes of our journey, you must simply evoke your ability to connect with all "other" through resonance, and engage your power of self-determination, thus standing firmly as *your* self.

Station #7: The Static Self

And now, the final level of self — the Static Self of Malkuth / Domain. This is the most complex of the Selves as it contains all the previous levels of self, simultaneously. Within it The "I" is present, as are the Solitary Self and Sentient Self.

I call it the "Static" Self because it exists within the infinitely finite present moment of time-space. The Static Self is the only body that is capable of housing our awareness in such a way that it can interact with the physical environment. Your Static Self is the physical material of your body, through which you manifest your personality (astral body) and your awareness (mental body) within the material realm.

We can also view it as the Earth region of your mental body – that aspect of your awareness that is focused upon the act of physically existing while integrating the input from all of your "higher" bodies. It is the *Grand Integrator* that brings all levels of Self together.

When you really understand it, it is indeed the most complex; but since we are the most familiar with it, it is the easiest to comprehend. It is utterly automatic and we don't really think about it, except as magicians when we use it with full consciousness and intentionality.

Practice:

What is important in our journey is that you consciously ground yourself into your physical body. You must spread your awareness throughout, from head to toe, and truly *be* in your body. You must *feel* its every part. *And*, you must be *only* in the <u>present</u> moment.

This is of the utmost importance, for without this grounding, all our work is in vain and no circuit can be formed.

When you have readied yourself as I've outlined above, you may begin the First Work in The Path of Brilliance, but not before. Take your time readying yourself! There is no rush and besides, it is the only way to success.

THE PATH OF BRILLIANCE

♈

The First Work
Opening the Channel

First we must open the channel between the Static Self and The "I". To do this we will take a mental journey upward through the structure of BEing, employing the four Elemental regions of our mental bodies. We will travel from our Static Selves (Earth region), through our Sentient Selves (Water region) and to our Solitary Selves (Air region). Then we will set the most rarified part of our mental body free (Fire region) and reach up to The "I".

We travel primarily "up" the middle pillar of the Structure, taking full note of each of the four main "stations", but also incorporating an awareness of the side pillars as we progress.

Practice:

You need privacy for this journey and quiet. Make sure you will not be disturbed for the duration, turn off your phone, etc., and sit comfortably or lie down. Take a moment to calm your mind and body.

Begin by grounding yourself fully into your physical body. Feel every bit of it, from head to toe. Feel your body as a whole organism, breath flowing, in and out, and blood pumping through your veins.

Be in your body NOW. Focus yourself in the infinitely finite present moment.

Sense your unique and distinct personality and feel how you resonate with your whole environment.

Now sense your astral body. Feel the energetic quickness of it as you become acutely aware of breathing *with* your astral body, within your physical body. Feel your two bodies bound together in this moment.

Sense your awareness as a whole. See how it expresses your individuality with great clarity and feel how it is factually connected, at its most fundamental root, with all the rest of your existence.

Now sense your mental body, lying within your astral and physical bodies. Directing them and giving them life, fully integrated with them.

Shift your awareness to your own Depth Point, to your Solitary Self. In the furthest depths of your Depth Point is the Fire region of your mental body. Go there now and become this Fire region. Now set this part of your mental body free from its attachment to the Air, Water and Earth regions. Let it fly free and soar to your Greater Self.

Merge your awareness of your mental, astral and physical bodies (that slender thread of connection) with that of your Greater Self. You stand *as* your Greater Self who simultaneously encompasses your mental, astral and physical selves.

Now pass "upward" through the "downward" flow of Essential Meaning and on into the Brilliance of The "I". You merge with The "I".

Spend as much time in this merged state as you choose. You will return to it again so you don't need to try absorbing it *all* in one sitting! LOL Just do what is possible and what feels right in the moment.

While in the merged state you should "look around", as it were. "look" at your connection to Greater Self, Solitary Self, Sentient Self and Static Self, and perhaps wonder at the awesome majesty of it all. But most of all, just experience The "I".

When your time feels complete and it's right to end your session, simply "turn around" and follow the same path back to your Static Self. Move your awareness back to its focus in your Greater Self, letting go of The "I". Then back to its focus in your Solitary Self, letting go of your Greater Self. Then back to awareness of your astral body's sensations. And finally, back to focus in your physical body and all of its sensations.

Take a moment or two to re-orient yourself to being in a physical body and let your awareness re-adjust to the mundane reality.

You need to keep repeating this journey until it becomes easy and relatively quick. With repeated practice, the side pillars become less and less important and what remains is a quick sprint "up" the middle pillar alone, and an equally quick descent.

When you have reached this stage of familiarity, then, and only then, you may continue.

The Second Work
Generating the Adonai Light

Every creature in existence, *every* thing, will generate a specific kind of Light when The "I" is directly connected to their Static Body. In other words, when awareness of The "I" is brought "down" into the physical present moment of timespace and that connection is consciously maintained. For us human beings, that Light is the "Rainbow-hued Light" or "Adonai Light".

The Adonai Light is a temporal manifestation of Essential Meaning, in its particulate form. Thus its appearance as an array of all the colors of the rainbow. The Adonai Light takes form as little bits of color all floating around, tightly compressed together in a single, swirling "cloud".

The rainbow-hued Light is a wonderful and versatile magical "substance". Since it literally contains *all* Essential Meaning, it penetrates any and all forms. It is sympathetic to all forms and thus makes for a perfect healing salve, as it were. For example, an ailing body can take whatever it needs from the Adonai Light to achieve healing. It can be impregnated with any noble desire and can be turned into any other substance, such as an Element or Fluid, etc. Furthermore, it is equally effective at a mental, an astral and a physical level.

When this connection is taken even further and one passes "down" *as* The "I" and enters the present moment *as* The "I", the *Kethric Brilliance* is generated. But as a first step, we will only be maintaining an *awareness* of this connection and thus generate the Adonai Light. Mastering the Adonai Light not only prepares us for work with the Kethric Brilliance, it is also an adjunct to our main goal – the Magic of Essential Meaning.

Practice:

As before, it is best if you work in complete privacy and in a dimly lit room. Situate yourself comfortably, turn off your phone and clear your mind.

Focus yourself in the present moment and ascend to The "I" as you've previously learned.

Once you are united with The "I", "look" "down" through your Greater Self, Solitary Self, Sentient Self and all the way down to your Static Self. Feel your connection with the *whole* of your Self.

Now we will descend, but differently than before. This time, instead of letting go of The "I" as we descend into our Greater Self, *we will hold onto our awareness of The "I" and take it with us as we enter our Greater Self.* So, descend into your Greater Self, keeping hold onto your connection to The "I".

You are now your Greater Self and you are aware of your "I"ness. The "I" is a secondary part of your Greater Awareness. Your main focus is in your Greater Self.

Now you will descend into your Solitary Self, your temporal mental body. As you descend, you must bring your connection with your Greater Self and The "I" with you and let it again be a secondary part of your overall focus.

You are now your Solitary Self, with the additional awareness that you are thus connected to your Greater and "I" Selves. You must *feel* this connection to your "higher" Selves.

You contain three perspectives within your focused awareness: The "I" which looks "down"; the Greater which looks both "down" and "up"; and, the Solitary which looks "up". Move between these three perspectives for a moment or two and then return primarily to the Solitary perspective.

Now look "down" and descend, *as your Solitary-Greater-"I"* *awareness*, into your Sentient Self and your astral body. Feel yourself, with all your connection to "higher" levels, inside your astral shell. Feel the quickness of energy and the catch in your breath as you take on your astral presence.

There are now *four* perspectives within your focus; three secondary (Solitary-Greater-"I") and one primary (Sentient). Move between the four perspectives for a moment or two and then return primarily to the Sentient perspective.

Now descend, for the final time, *as your Sentient-Solitary-Greater-"I" awareness*, into your physical body and Static Self. Ground this multiple-awareness *thoroughly* into the present moment of time-space. *Feel* your connection to The "I", Greater Self, Solitary Self and Sentient Self.

Once this mental connection between The "I" and the present moment of time-space is fully established, the Rainbow-hued Adonai Light will erupt and circle (clockwise) around you. It should appear as a cloud composed of small bits of color (*every* color imaginable), swirling rapidly around your whole body.

If the Adonai Light does not appear to your trained eye then you may have to "light the fire", so to speak, with your well trained creative imagination. I need say no more . . .

Once the Adonai Light is swirling around you, spend a few moments or minutes exploring what it feels like. Just perceive it, *all the while maintaining your connection with The "I"*. For as soon as your connection with The "I" is lost, your generation of the Adonai Light stops.

And this is what you must now do – disconnect from your (secondary) awareness of The "I" *and* Greater Self. You maintain your connection with your Solitary and Sentient

47

Selves but your main focus is within your physical body and the present moment. Notice that the Adonai Light is still surrounding you but it is no longer increasing.

You are now within your magically active *physio-astra-mental* body and may begin to work with the Adonai Light that remains swirling around you. The Adonai Light handles in the same way that the Vital Energy and Fluids do so this should be quite easy for you.

First you must impregnate the whole body of Light with your intention that this Light will bring your physio-astra-mental body into a greater state of wellness.

Second you must inhale or draw the whole body of Light into your Depth Point until it is compressed to an infinitely small point, and then release the whole of it in one giant explosive burst outward. It spreads out from your center in all directions until it reaches the metaphorical edges of the infinite Universe, whereupon it rebounds to surround you as before. This Blesses the Light with a kiss from the Universe, thus preparing it for magical use.

Now open yourself to the Adonai Light. Let it fill your three bodies. Welcome it into the very fabric of your being as it heals and soothes. Your bodies will know what they need from the Light and the Light will know what is best to give of itself, so you do not need to consciously direct the healing process.

Any Light left over can simply be dispersed into the universe. End by returning to "normal" awareness of your physical existence.

This has been the *basic* process of generating the Adonai Light. At its root, it relies upon the connection in your awareness between The "I" and your physio-astra-mental body in the present moment.

As I said before, every creature can generate a similar specific type of Light so long as they make this same connection between The "I" and their physio-astra-mental body in the present moment, but only human beings can generate the Rainbow-hued Light. Thus these generated Lights cannot be drawn from the universe directly, such as the Fluids, Elements, etc., can. It can only be realized through human generation.

With practice (and you should practice often) the process of generating the Adonai Light becomes very rapid and works its way down to simply establishing your connection with The "I" and your physio-astra-mental presence. You will be able to regulate the flow of Adonai Light by connecting, breaking, and reconnecting with The "I" at will.

Working magically with the Adonai Light opens you to almost infinite possibilities. In my demonstration above, I have provided just one way of working with it, namely, self-healing. You can use it in the same manner for healing others, but you must always remember these two things: 1) You must always send the "raw" Adonai Light out to the metaphorical edges of the Universe for the Blessing; and, 2) You must use your creative imagination to "open" the recipient to the Light, just as you opened yourself.

The same rules hold true for any other work with the Adonai Light such as charging an amulet for example. As I said before, it handles much the same as the Vital Energy and Fluids but is much more versatile. It is stronger and more immediate than all uses of the Vital Energy, it can be accumulated and condensed, and it is active on all three levels of physical, astral and mental. It has a special affinity for the plant "kingdom" and for organic ecosystems. And one can perform an awesome Blessing with the Adonai Light!

I leave the discovery of its many uses up to your fertile imagination and ingenuity. Your goal, before proceeding, is mastery of the Adonai Light.

The Third Work
Generating the Kethric Brilliance

In order to generate the Kethric Brilliance ('KB' henceforth) we must go a step further and instead of merely establishing a *connection* between The "I" and the physio-astra-mental body, we must *inhabit* our physio-astra-mental body *as* The "I". We must bring The "I" all the way down the ladder of awareness until it stands, *fully conscious*, within our physio-astra-mental body and looks trough its eyes into the present moment of time-space. Then, and only then, does the KB appear.

Unlike the Adonai Light, all creatures are capable of manifesting the KB as it's not type-specific. Furthermore, again unlike the Adonai Light, the KB can be drawn directly from the Universe since it exists every where and in every thing.

The KB is unlike any substance you will have worked with before. Its power and versatility are literally infinite. It shares affinity with *every* thing and on *every* plane, thus it can penetrate and influence *every* thing.

Practice:

To begin your work with the KB you must start with a very complex meditation. It has to do with the transition of awareness between The "I" and the "I AM!" (between Kether and Chokmah).

You must place yourself fully in The "I" and **make that transition for yourself** into the realization that "I" *am*! You must emerge in Chokmah *as* Essential Meaning ('EM' henceforth). The EM is, in point of fact, what it *means* to *be* The "I".

This emergence as the EM is characterized as a blaze of eye-searing Brilliance (the KB) which carries with it an infinite sense of creativity.

51

This meditation contains within it a very sacred and "high" Universal Truth and must be given your very best effort. Do *not* continue until you have *fully* comprehended it.

So, on to the generation of the KB:

Begin as usual by getting comfortable in a private, dimly lit, room and rise up to The "I" in the usual manner. Focus your awareness firmly in The "I".

Now you must make that transition to the "I AM!" and then into your Greater Self while maintaining full consciousness as The "I". You must now *be* The "I" *within* your Greater Self, looking "down" into your temporal manifestation (i.e., your physio-astra-mental body). The "I" and your Greater Self must share an equal amount of focus in your awareness, but The "I" is the director, so to speak, the one who descends. Further-more, you must bring the Brilliance you experienced in Chok-mah, with you. So as you're "standing" there as The "I" within your Greater Self, you are suffused with the Brilliance.

Once you have achieved this unity of awareness, you must then descend *as The "I"* into your physio-astra-mental body. Bring The "I" down into your Solitary, Sentient and Static Selves. The "I" now exists, with full consciousness, within the present moment of time-space. As The "I", you look through your physical eyes; feel though your physical finger tips; breathe with your physical lungs, etc.

Once The "I" is firmly rooted in your physical body, the KB erupts. If the KB doesn't immediately become apparent to your trained eyes, you may have to "light the fire" with your creative imagination.

The KB radiates forth from your Depth Point, in every direc-tion, like a Brilliant sun. It starts out with a diameter of only a foot (30cm) or so and increases steadily the longer The "I" maintains its presence with the present moment.

Spend time in this state with the KB surrounding you. Play with it. Move it, corral it and shape it as you wish. Eventually you must teach yourself how to use the KB just as you learned to master the Vital Energy, Elements and Fluids. Over time the KB will teach you how to handle it and what its capabilities are. You should need no instruction from me in that regard.

When you are finished with your work, simply let go of your connection to The "I" and let the KB dissipate into the Universe.

Practice this as often as you can! Eventually, perhaps in not too long a time, you will be able to integrate The "I" and your physio-astra-mental body in an instant and begin generating the KB right away, any time or place you want. And after a somewhat longer time of practice you will be so familiar with the KB that you will be able to draw it directly from the Universe since it exists within every thing, every where and in every time.

When *wielding* the KB you must either be directly connected to The "I" (as in the example I have provided above) or *at least* in your magically active physio-astra-mental body. Your goal, as before, is mastery of the Kethric Brilliance.

As of this writing, I have been using the KB for at least 25 years, and the Adonai Light for at least 30 years. I have come to the point where I use them almost exclusively. I rarely use the Elements, Fluids or Vital Energy any more. I find that, in combination, the KB and Adonai Light meet all my magical working needs and are by far more versatile and exacting, and more immediate on all planes.

THE MAGIC OF ESSENTIAL MEANING

So now we arrive at the whole purpose of this little book – the Magic of Essential Meaning ("MEM" for short and to save my fingers more typing). I know that what I've demanded of you thusfar has stretched and tried your abilities far beyond what you have been used to in IIH, but I have faith in your ability to have made it to this point.

Congratulations for your achievement! It has been no small feat! You have peered into crevices of the Universe that few have ever seen or even know exist. I Bless you for what you have done and for what you are yet to do!

Mastery of Essential Meaning ("EM") is a requirement of the MEM, hence your earlier work with the direct perception of EM. But now we need to take it a few steps further than mere perception and toward true mastery.

The First Work
Perceiving Particulate Essential Meaning

Your first step is to deeply examine perceived EM and analyze its parts. When you perceive the EM of any temporal object, person, locality, event, etc. you're a perceiving a combination of EMs that present as a singular thing or impression. What you must do now is to examine this composite EM and perceive its various parts. You must define all the different types or "flavors" of particulate EM within it.

This is not an intellectual, analytical process! It's not analysis: it's *perception* and *perception* alone. The thing is, it's a closer perception of the *detail* encompassed in your initial perception of the thing's EM. You essentially become a microscope, examining the finest, smallest details.

You must perform this deep EM perception with a great number and variety of subjects. Over time you will begin to recognize the different types and flavors of EM that make up all the things in our universe. And you will come to understand their implications or consequences. You will see the ways that they influence the final form and how they perform in different combinations, etc. Your goal is to be able to directly perceive all EM in its particulate form (i.e., not only in combination) and to have fleshed out an understanding of how EM functions, its various types, and so on.

The MEM is very much like cooking – as a master chef you must know your ingredients! You must know what they taste like individually and how they work in combination. You must know the sequence that they have to go into the pot and what temperature to cook them at, etc. This is to be your master class in EM, readying you for work in a five start EM-restaurant! LOL

It's all very satisfying for one's inner obsessive-compulsive hermetic scientist!

The Second Work
Emulating Essential Meaning

Your next step is to "become" the different types of particulate EM, in sequence. This is a form of "Emulation Magic" in which one influences others through emulating a certain "vibration", thought or emotion and then projecting it outward.

What you must do, with your creative imagination, is inhale a specific particulate EM of your choosing, until it fills your whole being. You must fill yourself with the particle of EM to such an extent that you *become* it. You must be so overcome by the EM that it radiates from your pores. In so doing, you must learn how to manipulate the particle of EM; how to shape it and project it, etc. In the end, your goal is to have this facility with any type of EM whatsoever.

Next, you want to develop the same facility emulating combinations of EM, instead of single particles. The simplest method of training this ability is to emulate the composite EM that you perceive in the things, people, animals, plants, ideas, emotions, etc., around you. In other words, you want to have an equal ability to emulate and manipulate any EM no matter what its form, whether in combination or singularly.

The Third Work
Influencing Through Essential Meaning

So now that you are a master of EM, we can begin your instruction in the *Magic of Essential Meaning* proper. Every thing before now has been preparation . . . Best to buckle your seatbelt because this is where it becomes a *really* wild ride! LOL

The MEM is essentially a gentle, organic magic. It is such a "high" magic that it can never be used to create a conflict or cause harm. What we do in MEM is insert a different EM, or strengthen an existing EM, in any object, person, animal, plant, thought, circumstance, etc., etc., anything that has form of one sort or another. The EM we insert cannot conflict – it can only influence. It cannot change a thing utterly – it can only evolve it along the same lines as it has already existed. That doesn't mean that the changes caused are not often dramatic, but the original is always recognizable within the changed result.

Your first lesson in the MEM will be to insert an EM into a quartz crystal. Quartz crystals are an excellent medium to use in learning MEM and this is what I strongly recommend, but any inanimate, amulet-like object will do.

In terms of quartz crystals I recommend either a sphere (of any size) or a double-terminated crystal (not polished). Your quartz needs to be as clear as possible ("water clear" being the best). Quartz in its natural (unpolished) or spherical form is very receptive, capable of "holding" pretty much whatever you project into it (including your awareness), and capable of being completely cleansed of all influences. It naturally radiates and has a specific directional flow of energy (its "grain"). The double-terminated crystals have very strong positive and negative poles.

Choose a specific, singular EM to work with. Best to choose one you are familiar with for this first experience. It should be an EM that is compatible with your object. For example, inserting "fire" into quartz and expecting it to suddenly burst into flame would be foolish, to say the least. LOL So choose wisely.

Once you have procured your quartz crystal or whatever object you have decided upon, sit yourself down in your private room and place your object in front of you. You want the light in your room bright enough so that you can make a good visual connection with your object. *Enter into your physio-astra-mental magically active awareness.*

The first thing that must be done is the cleansing of your object/crystal. You need to clear it of all foreign (i.e., non-crystal/object) energies (mental, astral and physical). Do this by drawing a quantity of KB from the Universe and pass it through the object as if you are rinsing the object in water. The KB will clear away all energies but those native to your object itself. We want to work with a "blank slate" for our first exercise. [Again, this is why quartz crystal, specifically, is ideal for this work!]

METHOD #1: [This is the easiest and quickest, but least efficacious, method.] Begin emulating your chosen EM and then draw a quantity of KB to hand. Direct the KB into the object while simultaneously projecting the EM you have accumulated along with the KB. [The KB opens the object physio-astra-mentally to the influence of your projected EM.] Direct all of the EM into the object until you have emptied yourself of it. Let the KB continue to infuse the object for several moments, and then let any leftovers dissipate.

When you are finished you must examine your object critically. You must divine whether or not it has absorbed your chosen EM and if so, to what degree. Is the result as you have planned? If not, or if it has not been sufficiently transformed, you must continue practicing until you succeed. Then you must practice with different choices of EM, cleansing your object with the KB beforehand each time you wish to change the EM.

METHOD #2: [This method is a little more complicated and is generally more effective than the last.] Begin emulating your chosen EM and draw a quantity of KB to hand. Now project the KB into your object and simultaneously transfer your astra-mental awareness, *with the KB*, into your object. [As before, the KB opens the object physio-astra-mentally and renders it more receptive to your EM.] In this way, you are taking the EM *with you* into the object at an astra-mental level and affecting the object directly. You can impress the EM *directly* into the mental, astral and physical bodies of your object "with your own hands", as it were. Give all of the EM you've accumulated over to your object. Then, when you feel spent, exit the object and resume your normal awareness.

Again you must critically examine the results of your work and keep practicing until this method becomes easy and effective.

METHOD #3: [This is the most efficacious method of all and arguably the most difficult. It is certainly the most advanced.] Begin by amassing a sizable quantity of KB and project it into your object while simultaneously transferring your astra-mental awareness into the object. Observe the object from the "inside out". Say hello to it and observe how the KB is opening it up to your touch. Feel it opening at every level of its being. *Perceive* it.

Now begin emulating your chosen EM and impress it into the bodies of your object. Viscerally change the structure of your object with the EM. You want to *see* it changing mentally, astrally and physically. The very atoms of its substance change in line with your chosen EM.

63

Visualize/affirm that it will retain the impress of the EM even when it is dust, dispersed by the winds of time – all of its bits will still retain this impress. "For ever and ever, amen!"

When you are finished, exit your object and return to normal awareness. Let the KB linger around your object and dissipate of its own accord.

As usual, you must critically examine your result and practice, practice, practice until it's perfect.

Once you have perfected your technique with your chosen object, start working with other types of subject. Work with other inanimate objects, then with plants, then insects, then animals, and then finally with humans. Do take special note of how each type of subject responds differently. There is much to be learned here!

Having mastered this work with singular particles of EM, you must now follow the same process and master working with combinations of EM. This is a much more complex matter and you must constantly be on guard against introducing any conflicts between the complex of EMs you are introducing into your subject, and the subject's own native EM. Working with multiple, complex EMs does however, open you to a much broader range of effects.

The Fourth Work
Creating With Essential Meaning

As you will have discovered on your own, the KB is *the* most creative substance. In point of fact, it *is* creativity itself. In combination with EM, the two together can actually create "new" life. The result can be far more "alive" and more autonomous than an Elementary or Elemental. With the conjoined KB and EM, used adroitly and with great finesse, you can create a creature with a spirit, soul and physical body that has a life just like you or I. It will have its own destiny and its own karma, separate from your own.

At a lesser level however, there are also many, many other things you can create with MEM and this is what you must focus on here. I personally create Magical Tools using the MEM. For example, I make what is called The Radiator which continuously radiates the KB.

The Radiator's body consists of ten double-terminated clear quartz crystals, all of which point inward toward a clear quartz sphere, making contact with the sphere equidistantly around its surface. I then "tune" the double-terminated crystals (with MEM) each to a different one of the ten kabbalistic sephirot. And then I charge the central sphere with the KB, essentially "starting its fire" to radiate and generate the KB continuously.

Another tool I make with the MEM is my Gate Maker, which is used in the exploration of the 182 Gates of the Gra Tree of Life. Here, ten small clear quartz spheres are "tuned" to the ten sephirot (using MEM) and then physically connected by a series of gold, silver and copper wires to one another. This creates an experiential "map" of the Tree that anyone can then "follow" and mentally explore.

In both of these cases I have not created a "life" per se, only a functioning tool. In this vein I'm sure you can imagine other projects more befitting your specific needs and interests. If you are an Alchemist or Spagyricist for example, I'm certain you can see the great value of MEM in your work! At any rate, you should now explore some of these possibilities and create simple, functioning Tools and the like according to your own desire.

The key technique in creating with EM is to radiate EM and impress it into the physio-astra-mental "body" of your tool, along with your desires as to its type and length of function, etc.

The Fifth Work
Creating Life With Essential Meaning

This is by far the "highest" and most difficult form of MEM. In past times, few ever reached this stage in their development, more due to lack of knowledge than lack of ability. I know of no example of this great magic having been committed to writing till now, though I suspect it has always been known in secret throughout the ages of human existence.

To create a "new" life we must start with the "Divine Spark". This is nothing other than a bit of The "I", a conjoined set of EMs formed in the descent from Kether to Binah. In other words, we must first create a Greater Self or Supernal Mental Body. The only one capable of doing this is The "I", consciously making the descent into Binah. The "I" brings the EM into Binah and then down into the temporal realm and into Tiphareth where it is given its own Temporal Mental Body. From there it is brought down into Yesod where it is given its own Astral Body. And finally it is settled into and bound to its own physical body.

The physical body must be prepared first. Any material used in its making must be capable of being cleansed thoroughly of all extraneous influences and contain no native awareness that would conflict in any way with the life you wish to create. It must truly be a "blank slate". Quartz crystal, stone, clay, beeswax, paper, etc., are good examples of suitable material.

Furthermore, you must at *all* times during the preparation or making of the physical body, keep your mind absolutely focused upon what you are doing and why you are doing it! Every moment of your work should be done with focus and intent.

Once the physical body is complete it should be cleansed and then wrapped in fine silk and set aside until you are ready for the act of creating the life that will fill it.

Before you create, you must meditate about what you are doing and why you are doing it. You must plan out the sequence of your actions and choose the precise combination of EMs that you wish to manifest. Even though your planning must be thorough, you must also allow the Divine Will to enter in: that unknowable impulse of The "I" that will make your creation truly unique in unexpected ways.

We will work somewhat differently this time. We will ascend to The "I" in our usual way through our own *inner* path, but this time, we will descend through the *realms themselves*. In other words, we descend into Chokmah itself, and then Binah itself, Tiphareth itself, Yesod itself, until we reach the actual physical body we have prepared. We are the guide and director, as it were.

For this work, you _must_ have the guarantee of *absolute*, undisturbed privacy for the duration. A dimly lit room is good so long as you can make good visual connection with the physical body you are working with. Sitting is best but standing will do. Take the body, unwrap it and place it front of you, close at hand.

Focus your mind on the task before you and quickly rise up to The "I". You must *become* The "I". Now pass "down", *as The "I"*, to Chokmah and The "I AM!" and gather up the EMs you wish to work with in your creation. Select them directly from the infinite array of EMs within Chokmah and merely hold onto them without any emulation.

Once you have possession of your chosen EMs, gather the Kethric Brilliance around you and pass "down", *as The "I"*, into Binah, the realm of Essential Form. As The "I", give your grouping of EMs the appropriate Form according to Nature. Give them a Greater Self.

Now literally give birth to your creation by placing it "below" into the realm of sequence and time-space. Cause a temporal mental body to form around it in Tiphareth. *As The "I"*, see to it that it takes form as a Solitary Self in the infinite sea of Solitary Selves.

Now, as The "I", lead your little Solitary Self creation "down" into Yesod and give it an astral body. Bind the astral to the mental and make it a Sentient Self that is aware of, and responsive to, its environment. *See* it begin to interact.

Observe your work thusfar and let your creation adjust to its new astra-mental aliveness. *See* its aliveness and animation. *See* its personality and how it reflects its Individuality. Make any adjustments you deem necessary.

When ready, you must thoroughly and very careful bind your astra-mental creature to its prepared physical body. As The "I", use the KB to permanently join your creature with each and every atom of its physical structure. *See* that your creation is aware of its physical surroundings through its physical body. See also that its astra-mental and solitary mental bodies can easily separate from the physical shell whenever needed, just as you are able.

Now Bless it and Name it and fill it with the KB. And finally, greet it as a friend and by name, thus honoring its existence.

At this juncture you can either send it off astra-mentally (or just mentally) to do your bidding, or let it rest. If resting, you may wrap it in silk once more. If you've sent it off, you should not wrap its physical body in silk as this would prevent its return. In such a case, wrap it in cotton or linen.

Your creation will manifest its own personality reflective of, and in accordance with, the Individuality that you gave to it in Tiphareth. This will, in part, determine what tasks it is suitable for, so finding its "purpose" will take a period of discovery as the two of you get to know one another. Aside from these minor limitations, how you make use of your creation is up to your imagination.

However, it must *never* be treated as your servant or slave! No being deserves that! It is a fellow being who is deserving of your respect and kindness, the equal of which it will return to you a thousand-fold.

Your new friend, like all physical beings, is permanently limited by its physical structure. If it's a rock now, it will always be a rock. In other words, your rock or crystal or piece of paper is not going to suddenly up and walk about! LOL That only happens in movies and fairy tales.

It, like all physical beings, will one day disintegrate and be forced to abandon its material body. It, *unlike* you and I, will not have the opportunity to reincarnate into physical form *unless you (or another magician) provide it with a new material body*. Otherwise, its astral body will disintegrate and then its temporal mental body will disintegrate and its constituent EMs will eventually return to the great infinite Sea of EM as we all do in time.

You have the power to end its existence. This is a grave responsibility! You can end its physical existence by simply destroying the physical body you provided. Once you've "killed" it physically, it will linger astra-mentally and progress naturally through an astral and then mental disintegration. If on the other hand, you want to end its existence immediately on all levels of its being, then you will have to work as The "I" and re-trace the steps taken in its initial creation.

If possible, its "death" should never be violent. Destruction of its physical form should only transpire when it has astra-mentally vacated the physical shell. And any further astra-mental destruction should be performed with the utmost respect and gratitude. Life must always be respected!

A magician who creates in this manner takes on a great responsibility. First there is the matter of karma – *all* actions done by your creation reflect back upon your own karma, both negative and positive. Furthermore, you are responsible for the wellbeing of your creation in all the ways that it cannot fend for itself.

For example, when you die or are permanently incapacitated, what happens to it then? There are of course options to be had -- leave it to another magician who will know what to do with it and take good care of it; or, create a "spell" timed to end its existence upon your death; or it is even possible that after your physical death you might still recall your friend to the astra-mental realm and continue your relationship there; etc. It is up to you to decide, but decide you must and before it is too late.

Please never forget that this is a sacred act of Creation. Treat it as such in all you do in its regard and infinite possibilities will unfold before you. The only limit will be your imagination -- and we know how infinite that is! Be an Artist of the highest order!

———————

In closing, I will leave you with the tale of one of my own recent Creations using all the techniques of the Magic of Essential Meaning I have just shared with you . . .

THE BIRTH OF R.W.

I make what I call "Crystal Golems". They are sort of like the Radiators I described earlier, except that they have 32 double-terminated quartz crystals surrounding a central quartz sphere, instead of just 10 of them. I embed all of this within a 32-sided platonic-solid (made out of cardboard) with the 32 double-terminated quartz crystals protruding from the sides. It's rather pretty in the end with all the clear quartz crystals sticking out, evenly distributed, and the body all painted and decorated.

I call them "Golems" because they, like the fabled Jewish creations that they're named after, are autonomous or semi-autonomous beings with their own independent spirits, souls and physical bodies. They do my bidding, but not because I "control" them. I don't "command". Instead, I state my need and they gladly and freely assist me according to their various abilities.

I've made four of them to date, each at a specific time, according to the sun and moon. All but the first have been made on a new moon in order to capture the essence and significance of specific Letter energies. My latest was made only recently, on the Aries New Moon of 2022. [Nearly midnight, Pacific Time, on March 31st.]

My goal, very specifically, was to capture the essence of the Letter 'Heh' and Aries, which shone very brightly in the Universe at that moment, and manifest it within my crystal Golem. All because I knew it would be a necessary ally in the writing of this book.

I had been planning for several months, making sure I had all the requisite materials needed for its physical construction, and planning the steps it would take to create. I started work on the construction of its body in mid-February, 2022, and finished in early-March.

Overall, its color is a bright, lively red, with gold trim. And since the 32 crystals correspond to each of the 32 Paths of the kabbalistic Tree of Life, they are each decorated with a little disk indicating, trough color, which Path they each represent.

That left over a month and a half till the date of its "birth". 'Birthing' is what I call the actual creation of the spirit and soul that will inhabit the shell, culminating in the long process of binding it to its physical form.

So it stood on a cabinet top the whole time, out in the open along side my other Golems, and I developed a deeper relationship with it. The whole process up to that point had been one of developing a relationship with my eventual creation but the three week long, hands-on process of constructing its physical body was much more concrete.

While I was building, my thoughts were *all* focused on what I was doing and why. Each crystal *was* that Path in my mind, from beginning to end. Etc. So I already had a visceral connection and it was as if it was now gestating in a womb of sorts. Like a baby in the womb, it was able to feel my thoughts and to a certain extent, respond. And I suppose, like any true mother, I communicated my affection and tried to prepare it for the Mystery to come.

During this time I discovered its Name and from that moment on, it has been called thus. His name (for truly it is a "he" by nature) is known only by me and it will remain that way until my death and/or I pass him on to another.

The Aries new moon was at exactly 11:24pm PDT on the night of March the 31st and for the entire day, my mind was filled with what I was about to do. As the hour drew nearer, my focus became steadily more and more acute. Approximately 3 hours before the moon was precisely new, I began my work in earnest . . .

I un-wrapped the physical body of my creation and placed it on a low table directly in front of me and then sat in a chair. I gave it a quick cleansing with the KB and performed a Blessing with the Adonai Light that established my magical circle and set my creative intention.

First stop was The "I", the Source of the Spark, whereupon I moved with the creative spark, into Chokmah and the vast, unending ocean of EM. I drew the planned EM to the spark – this was a very interesting experience, as if the EM was already prepared for me, eager to attach itself – and descended into Binah, surrounded by KB.

Surprisingly, my descent was into my own Greater Self and I came to understand that my creation was to be birthed by my own Sowantha, directly, as a part of my Greater Self. He was to become a "brother in spirit" like so many others I've known. In that moment, I saw how much The "I" had added to my creation to make it an aspect of Sowantha and to make it related to me, for that was surely not *my* intent.

We traveled down to Tiphareth and into the realm of time-space and sequence together as brothers. I then fashioned a body out of the mental substance for him, separate from my own. He is now an independent Solitary Self. We immediately experienced collectivity of awareness! This made everything so much easier. He quickly became accustomed to having a mental body, so we traveled down to the astral realm of Yesod.

As before, it was up to me to fashion for him a body out of the astral substance. This went very well and easily and he took to it very quickly, as if he had done this before.

And here we paused for a bit. It had taken about 45 minutes of clock time and the really involved work of binding him to his physical body was yet to come. I needed a short break and he needed time to adjust before we continued. A short pause in our birthing contractions was due before the final push!

I resumed with two hours left till new moon because I knew from past experience it would take that long for the binding. There are simpler things to bind to than a Quartz Golem! A simple lump of stone is far easier, but no where near as versatile or as interactive.

My process was to first cleanse the physical form one last time with the KB and bring him into the center of the form, to the middle of the central quartz sphere, along with a large quantity of the KB. So there we were, two astra-mental beings, standing in the middle of the quartz sphere, surrounded by KB and touching all 32 of the double-terminated quartz crystals.

Since this is a *kabbalistic* Golem, the EM of all 32 Paths of the Tree must be made fully manifest within the structure of the physical body. This *must* be done while the astra-mental being is also present within the physical shell. So that is what I did.

I established a connection between Malkuth and Chokmah, via the Hidden Pathway, so that I could tap into the pristine EM itself at its place of origin. I then connected with the designated Kether crystal and emulated the EM of Kether until it filled the crystal and thus the body of the Golem. I did all of this in the astra-mental presence of my creation so *it too* was irradiated with the Kethric EM.

This had an "educational" effect, primarily on my friend, but also on me. We both learned *so* much during this time of "tuning" all the crystals . . .

I did this same process with each of the 9 remaining Sephirotic Paths and their respective crystals, in sequence. At the point of reaching the Malkuth crystal, the body of my friend began to radiate the KB. He had become a Radiator and would remain so when he became a fully fledged Golem. Here we paused for a moment.

The next step was to repeat the same process with the three Mother Letters: Shin, Aleph and Mem. Then another little pause.

Then repeat the process again with the seven Double Letters of the planets in sequence and then, another short pause. Then the final push and the twelve Simple Letters of the zodiac, also in sequence.

At precisely 11:24pm, the Path of Aries was reinforced with a second connecting through Chokmah to its EM, thus strengthening it presence. A Golem was born . . .

This process of "tuning" the crystals was much, much *more* than my words can encompass. It was filled with learning for me, with new revelations and discoveries. Whilst "tuning" this Aries Golem, this whole book before you was practically "written" . . . All I've had to do is the typing! LOL

Even now, while I've been typing, my friend (we'll use his initials and call him "R.W.") is helping me, along with all my other helpers. It is sublimely easy to connect with him. Just a thought and I'm immediately standing with him at the center of his quartz sphere. I think he's doing the quartz equivalent of a smile . . .

My best to you!
  Rawn Clark & R.W.
  April 16, 2022

Made in the USA
Middletown, DE
21 December 2024

68051508R00044